The Guide to
Real Subversive Soldiering

Also by Robert Holles

Novels

Now Thrive the Armourers
The Bribe Scorners
Captain Cat
The Siege of Battersea
Religion and Davey Peach
The Nature of the Beast
Spawn
I'll Walk Beside You
Sunblight

Humour

The Guide to Real Village Cricket

The Guide to
Real Subversive Soldiering

ROBERT HOLLES

Illustrated by Roy Raymonde

GUILD PUBLISHING
LONDON

Photoset by Rowland Phototypesetting Ltd
Bury St Edmunds, Suffolk
Printed and bound in Great Britain by
Biddles Ltd, Guildford and King's Lynn

CONTENTS

INTRODUCTION

At the age of fourteen I was removed from the genial scholastic environment of a grammar school by my parent, (an ex-sergeant major) and transferred, at the stroke of a pen, to the military ambience of boy service in the Regular Army. It was something of a traumatic experience. I was suddenly conveyed to a boarding establishment where the teaching staff were bawling, prancing disciplinarians, and my fellow pupils had such a scant command of the English language that they were prone to using the same word as noun, verb, adverb and adjective all in the same sentence.

My particular intake were to be trained as armourers, so I was compelled, for the next three years, to learn how to repair weapons although I had no mechanical skill or inclination in this direction whatsoever. Lessons were conducted at a frenetic pace – the most heinous crime seemed to be standing still. Contemplation was a chargeable offence. The discomfort was acute and the whole place reeked of punishment, official and unofficial. It wasn't long before I decided that the military milieu was not my scene. I wished to retire from it and concentrate on my basic ambition to become a writer, in more reflective surroundings. But there remained the small matter of fifteen years of compulsory military service to complete.

I realised that the first priority was to find a means of surviving the furious tide of military indoctrination – I could see what had happened to past victims all around me, and it wasn't a pretty sight. Obviously the frontal assault wasn't a good idea – the opposition was much too powerful, and I was outnumbered by about 160,000 to one. So I became a subversive, resisting the system from within and below, and eventually I managed to survive.

But not without getting very close to the brink. A year or two after entering man service I was awarded my second stripe. I began to feel a surge of power. I actually enjoyed marching squads of men, watching them move in cohesion to my fatuous commands . . . 'left right left right left . . . halt . . . about turn!' etc. A couple of weeks after my promotion I was guard commander for the first time. When I took over the guardroom from the regimental police, I was asked to sign for a prisoner, but he wasn't in the cells. I was told that he'd been allowed out for a couple of hours and would be back a bit later. (Apparently he was a decent sort of bloke, and had promised not to run away.) I insisted that he be found and clapped inside again immediately.

Later that night it was my duty to close the bar of the NAAFI at 10 p.m. I went round there ten minutes early and ordered the staff to close on time, and I sat alone at a table to make sure that this instruction was carried out. A few moments later I was struck, just above the ear, by a stale rock cake. When I had recovered from the shock I glared around the bar. There were about a dozen occupants. Three of them were deeply involved in earnest conversation . . . another was engrossed in the *Daily Mirror*. The remainder, arms folded, were staring fixedly at the walls.

I chuntered over this incident for the next few days, then realised that I'd been dragged back from the abyss. From that time I never again tried to grow into a good solider. (If whoever it was slung that rock cake wants to own up, I'd like to offer him my heart-felt thanks, and compliment him on his accuracy.) I went on to achieve the rank of sergeant and a reputation which is still discussed at Old Comrades' Reunions – I was the scruffiest sergeant the British Army had known, and the only one who'd never been heard to give anyone an order.

In the present climate of high unemployment there must

be many young blokes in uniform who wouldn't be wearing it if jobs were not so scarce elsewhere. Many will find it difficult to hang on to their unique character and personality. I devote the following pages to them, in the hope that my own fifteen years of reluctant service in the ranks will provide a few useful hints on how to survive the pitfalls and perils of the military regime, avoid indoctrination, and emerge as an individual.

ENLISTMENT

A great deal of care must be taken at the enlistment stage to prevent one's military career becoming an utterly disastrous – and perhaps terminal – experience. The ambition should be to sort yourself out a cushy number with a chance of the odd overseas tour (strictly for showing the flag), and with as little risk of danger or discomfort as possible. Thus outfits such as the SAS, Commandos, or the Army Physical Training Corps shouldn't be considered, and the Paratroops scrupulously avoided. It may sound easy to jump out of an aeroplane at 5,000 feet, but it has to be remembered that sometimes parachutes fail to open and, due to modern methods of economic farming, haystacks are few and far between.

The Guards regiments are also to be eschewed, unless of course one happens to be a masochist with a penchant for being bawled at from dawn until dusk, when not marching back and forth from a sentry box in fancy dress in front of hordes of Japanese tourists with popping Nikons. Better to be a cook in the Army Catering Corps – always in the warm and never short of a good nosh-up. The Ordnance Corps is also a useful number as dishing out stores to those who have the necessary documentation bestows a satisfying sense of power. The Royal Engineers can be rewarding too, provided of course one can avoid the section which specialises in laying mines (and collecting them afterwards when they're no longer wanted). Don't despise the good old plodding infantry, though I'd put it rather well down the list. Never overlook the Royal Artillery either – if you should happen to find yourself at the sharp end you'll always be at least five miles away from the nearest gook.

One of the major obstacles towards ending up in the mob of your choice is the guideline for recruiting officers laid down by General Sir Eustace Eadie-Wemyss in 1906, and still in force today:

The skills and experience accumulated in civilian life by the applicant must be considered in obverse relationship to his future deployment as a soldier.

(The Eadie-Wemyss Edict)

It is therefore essential for the potential recruit, when he duly reports to the Army Careers Information Office, to fit himself up with a false background, and he should never put his first choice of regiment on top of the list.

'What sort of work are you doin' now, son?'

'I'm a qualified dental mechanic.'

'I see. What sort of unit would you like to join?'

'I was thinkin' about the Army Dental Corps.'

'Sorry, no vacancies there for at least five years.'

'What about the Military Police, then?'

'They're well over establishment already.'

'Intelligence Corps?'

'You need three foreign languages for that.'

'I've got an 'O' level in French.'

'Tell me something more about yourself. What does your father do for a living?'

' 'E's on the dole. But I have got a brother who plays in goal for Queen's Park Rangers.'

'Oh really? Er . . . why don't you take a seat over there? Should be a cup of coffee comin' up in a minute. Now er . . . Royal Corps of Signals . . . that any good to yer?'

THE SHARP END

Danger – keep out!

Regular soldiers don't often find themselves crouching in foxholes, or charging across rugged terrain spewing chunks of phospher-bronze at everything in sight, unless they're just rehearsing for something they hope will never happen. The problem is that little bushfire operations do tend to spring up from time to time – such as the Falklands business – which pose a serious threat to life and limb. Peacekeeping forces also qualify for a high risk rate of insurance, particularly if the local militias aren't over enthusiastic about the peace being kept.

It is essential, therefore, to try and avoid getting involved in such situations. (After all, who needs to finish up as a name on a hunk of Portland stone?) The best way is to ensure that you are one of the two or three back-up troops supporting every front-line soldier sitting in a tent about a thousand miles away and sorting out their mail.

Another sensible precaution is to join a religious sect which forbids the adulteration of the blood of the faithful by squirting in vaccine, etc. When you refuse your inoculations prior to being drafted to a place where the ironmongery is in serious use, it won't make you exactly popular. But after all, a man is entitled to stand by his religious beliefs, above all else. Isn't he?

But if all else fails and you find yourself in a situation where the opposition is in earnest there are a few simple rules which should be followed. When digging your foxhole, for example, make it that extra bit deeper so that you don't

13

have to stoop while keeping your head down, and carry a simple periscope in your kit. And when you go out on patrol into enemy territory, start tying your bootlaces as the others are about to move off, so that you'll be last in the file.

Otherwise, keep your fingers crossed and don't forget to say your prayers.

QUEEN'S REGULATIONS

Every recruit discovers, at an early stage, that he has swapped his civil liberties for a set of rules known as Queen's Regulations. These allegedly constitute the army's bible – the book of words governing every aspect of military life from Baptism, (Certificate and Record of) to Funerals (Pall, by whom to be borne at) – and cover some 1,697 paragraphs and twenty-nine appendices.

They are revised from time to time, but rather slowly. There is a team of ex-officers, somewhere under the cellars of the War Office, who are responsible for keeping them up to date. The ex-officers employed in this task have to know the regulations by heart, which takes a lifetime of service, so they are normally appointed when they are about sixty-five, and the average age of these old fusspots is eighty-two and five months.

Occasionally a paragraph is spotted which has clearly become redundant, such as:

Commanders of troops occupied on guard duties in ships transporting convicted felons to Botany Bay or Van Diemen's Land, will ensure that the troops are fed on separate mess decks from the prisoners.

It is clear that this item needs to be withdrawn, but it can't be simply taken out otherwise the numbers of all the paragraphs coming after it will have to be changed, and the whole edition reprinted at enormous cost. The revision team put their heads together for something to replace it with, like . . .

Soldiers escorting prisoners on civil aircraft will be given a separate, and where circumstances allow, superior meal to that supplied to the prisoner they are escorting.

But one geriatric points out that this would be impracticable since it would be necessary to write to every civil airline in the world to ask if they were willing to provide such facilities, and the cost of the stamps alone would take them past their annual budget. So they fall back on the old reliable formula, which explains why you find entries such as:

(238–257) Reserved.
(388–398) Reserved.
(767–768) Reserved.

The team has been deliberating for twenty years over one paragraph, dealing with civil disturbance, which doesn't quite seem to make sense:

Care will be taken to fire only on those persons who are seen to be implicated in the disturbance. To fire over the heads of a crowd has the effect of favouring the most daring and guilty, and of sacrificing the less daring, and even the innocent.

'But Cartwright . . . I say, look here, dammit . . . how can you favour the guilty, and sacrifice the innocent, if you're only firing over the heads of the buggers?'

*

These days QRs are somewhat redundant, a set of archaic guidelines for officers to fall back on and use to their best advantage, or ignore when they happen to be inconvenient. Yet every squaddie should have a copy in his locker for the entertainment value, and the occasional bits of useful advice on sexual matters:

A report will be at once forwarded to the War Office if any remount turns out to be a wind sucker or crib biter, or shows signs of any particular vice . . .

16

EXIGENCIES OF THE SERVICE

This phrase first appeared in the *Manual of Military Law* about ninety years ago. It was intended to cover the absence of an officer on the board of a court martial who had suddenly found himself committed to business elsewhere, such as the Siege of Kut, or was suffering from a monumental attack of migraine following the annual regimental dinner celebrating the anniversary of Minden Day.

> *Major Postlethwaite has been excused by the president, due to the exigencies of the service.*

Unfortunately the term has since been used to serve the convenience of military authority in just about every conceivable aspect of army life. Imagine that some psychopath of a CO decides to lay on an all-night exercise by his battalion in order to 'get rid of the cobwebs' at about five hours' notice. A squaddie in 'A' Company has just taken his wife to the maternity ward, and wants to hang around for a while to see what emerges. But his Company Commander tells him, 'I'm sorry about this, Hobbs, but there are absolutely no exemptions from this exercise. I'm afraid you'll have to put it down to the exigencies of the service.'

You are just about to go on a month's leave, with your flight booked to Benidorm. The day before you go you're informed that an inspection team is arriving next week to examine the ammunition and you just happen to be in charge of the ammo stores. Sorry old mate, put it down to the exigencies of the service.

'In any case, Corporal Briggs, you realise of course that leave is a privilege, not an entitlement.'

'Sah!'

You are due to marry the hottest bit of property in Chislehurst, in two weeks' time. Everything's laid on. Her Dad's not short of a few bob and there's over a hundred on the guest list, including half a dozen of your mates from 6 Platoon. Stacks of champers after, followed by the little drive down to the cottage on the edge of Dartmoor. Then the Dorsets get switched to Cyprus overnight and you've got to take their place in South Armagh.

'I'm afraid we'll need you for the baggage party, Sergeant Silcock, you'll just have to put it down to the exigencies of the service. But I dare say, in a couple of months perhaps . . .'

'Sah!'

So 'exigencies of the service' has come to mean withdrawal of privileges, as the CO sees fit, for any reason whatsoever. The young soldier will quickly discover that there is no real defence against them – they're like bullets, you can't see them coming. The only defence is to keep your head down and hope they'll pass harmlessly by – apart of course from going over the wall and leaving a note for the sergeant-major:

Sir. Due to the exigencies of the service, I have decided to take a voluntary and immediate discharge from the service of HM Forces with effect from the above date. I am willing, under the circumstances, to abrogate any accrued pension rights – perhaps you would be kind enough to notify the appropriate authority. Yours, etc . . . Mr J. K. Pickard (Pte, Retd)

VOCABULARY

Rudyard Kipling was among the first to observe that the British squaddie had developed a language of his own. These days the unique language of the barrack room still retains fragments of Arabic and Urdu from the days of the Empire, bolstered by the popular scatology of the last fifty years or so, and garnished with a few basic Anglo-Saxon mots.

Thus women are still described as bints. A crazy man is dulally, McNoon, or bomb-happy. Money is ackers or gilt. Medals are gongs, and 'Juldee!' means 'get a move on!'

Shagnasty is the term for an unpopular superior. (Also bollockchops or bastard-features.) Mungarear is simply food, and has no connection with digestive disorders. A rectum is referred to as a ring, jacksie, or duff.

Even terms of endearment from close companions can sometimes sound a bit rough and ready, such as, 'Ey Arthur, is that right you managed to skive off range practice, you crafty old tit?'

Or:

'Ey Wally, you snivelling snotgobbling squeal from an imprisoned turd . . . what are you?' – which can be an expression of genuine affection, provided it's accompanied by a smirk and a comradely thump between the shoulder blades.

The new recruit shouldn't have too much trouble in assimilating this military patois, in any case he has no choice. But serious problems may arise when he is confronted with the nomenclature system of the stores identification lists. The army uses an enormous amount of gear, (courtesy of the taxpayer) and all of it is annotated in various stores lists. The particular style of the vocabulary used is always arse-about-face. So that in a list of machine-gun parts, for example, you will find: *Cover ejection opening, (instead of ejection opening cover) screw protector foresight, pin locking body, pin retaining pin locking body, and spring pin retaining pin locking body.*

The description given to each item is very explicit, so that a distinction can easily be made even for articles which have a similar use:

Sheets, ground, other ranks for the use of.
Sheets, ground, officers.
Coats, rain, Burberry, officers for the use of.

In fact, the other ranks' groundsheets button round the neck, and double up as raincoats. The problem is that when they are used as groundsheets there's a big hole in the middle where the head goes through. Sheets, ground, officers, however, don't have this particular feature. They are all groundsheet, and perfectly match the ground area covered by tents, officers. These are considerably larger than tents, other ranks, which exist only in theory – they are always marked NA (not available) in the stores list. The same with beds, camp, and bags, sleeping, which are normally only issued to officers, although the ordinary squaddie will occasionally be issued with a net, mosquito, always provided that he is serving in a region which is untroubled by insects of this species.

The problem is that this reverse vocabulary has a tendency to grow on one by stealth. It starts to become dangerous when you finger the piece of plastic in your headgear and begin to think of it as a 'badges, cap'. This is one of the early signs of indoctrination, and must be fiercely resisted.

I came across an advanced case of this sort while stationed at a REME workshop in the tropics. Because of the steamy heat I was in the habit of taking a flask of coffee to work every morning – I carried it in a small canvas bag. It seems

22

that a quantity of tools had begun to disappear from the workshops and the CO came to the rather obvious conclusion that they were being nicked by the rank and file and smuggled out in bags of various descriptions. So he ordained that in future nobody (except officers) would be permitted to take a bag in or out of the workshops. I wasn't particularly happy about this edict. For one thing I didn't care to be branded as a thief and, more importantly, a flask is an awkward item to carry about on its own. I therefore went to the equipment

repair shop and asked a craftsman in there to make me a flask carrier out of strips of webbing. A couple of days later I appeared at the workshops gate carrying my flask in its flimsy container. The CSM, skulking around the gatehouse, accosted me. 'You can't bring that in 'ere,' he said.

'Why not? It's not a bag, it's just a couple of strips of webbing sewn together.'

'Right, we'll soon find out about that,' he replied grimly. 'We'll ask the Workshop Officer.'

He led me across to the Workshop Office.

The Workshop Officer, Lieutenant Pridgeon, had prematurely white hair and a thin head which was always inclined forward, like a turtle's. Everybody wondered why he could be so old without having made captain. He kept us waiting for the statutory ten minutes, then admitted us to his office. As the sergeant-major outlined the situation he listened earnestly, then he took the flask and its accoutrements and turned them over in his hands, nodding and sucking his teeth. The CSM and I stood there sweating a little, waiting for his momentous decision. It was a long time coming. Finally he said, 'Yes, it's a bag all right. It's a bag carrier, flask transporting for the purpose of.'

This statement saddened me deeply. I knew that I was in the presence of a man who had little or no future. About five years later Pridgeon did get his third pip, but he was bowler-hatted almost immediately. The War Office discovered that there was a huge surplus of captains who were blighting the promotion prospects for those below, and it was decided to get rid of a thousand or two.

I met Pridgeon again some twenty years later, long after my own demobilisation, when I dropped into a cafe on the outskirts of Romford for a quick snack. Pridgeon was behind the counter taking the orders. I recognised him instantly. He scarcely seemed to have aged at all, still looked a boyish sixty.

'What would you like?' he enquired.

'Eggs poached, sausages pork, mushrooms devilled, and potatoes french fried . . . oh and have you got any sauce Thousand Island?'

He looked at me sourly.

HAIRCUTS

According to Queen's Regulations 'the hair of the head will be kept short.' In terms of instructions to the barber, this means 'a short back and sides'.

Military authority has traditionally been paranoic about haircuts, long hair being equated with a rebellious nature. Nor is there any strict interpretation of the letter of the law. A skinhead, for example, would receive instant attention from his sergeant-major for departing from the norm. 'If you don't let your 'air grow lad, I'll make you sweat, my word I will!'

A short haircut can be something of a traumatic experience for the fledgeling soldier, since it sets him apart from the civilian breed from which he has so recently sprung – especially when he is off-duty and wearing normal togs. If this bothers him, he's on the right track. If it doesn't, he's in serious danger. It means that he's already been so brainwashed by his instructors that he seriously believes that a fit and well-trained young soldier with bristles like new-mown wheat is one of the princelings of society, while the pasty-faced civilian yobbos who foregather in the local boozer represent its garbage. (The yobbos consider exactly the reverse is true, since they decline to take orders from anybody, and they could have a point.)

Although I was never interested in the cosmetic possibilities of particular hair styles, I found this mania for short hair irksome throughout the whole of my service. To maintain a short back and sides demanded a fortnightly visit to the barber's shop, which I considered both inconvenient and

unnecessary. I had more important things to do with my time.

I eventually adopted the policy of waiting until I was ordered to get a haircut, before actually getting one. In this way I found I was able to extend the period between visits to the barber's to something like five or six weeks. And on a few occasions, in backwoods units where no sergeant-majors were on the prowl, I even managed to get it curling over the collar.

On one occasion in Nigeria, I recall building up quite a substantial coiffure before I was accosted by the CSM – a man who had the features of a gargoyle designed to illustrate the excesses of both lechery and alcoholic indulgence.

'Get your 'air cut, sergeant,' he commanded.

'If you say so, Jimmy.'

We had been on Christian name terms since I had helped to carry him back to his sweatbox one night after the christening of somebody's promotion to staff sergeant in the mess.

That same evening I summoned a Nigerian barber to my quarters and paid him to crop my locks while I chatted idly to a fellow sergeant from the adjoining billet. Next morning I left one of those locks in an envelope on Jimmy's desk in order to demonstrate that his instruction had been duly carried out. For some inexplicable reason, this thoughtful gesture seemed to get up Jimmy's nose. He responded by sticking me on a fizzer for not having had a haircut, after he had ordered me to do so.

I went up before Captain Dolbear (known as Dolly Bear), an officer who was famous for having a twenty-one-inch

neck, so that all his shirts had to be imported from some establishment in Camberley which catered for the sartorial needs of oversized officers. He was also reputed to be very good with his hands, and could take a bicycle pump to pieces and put it together again, so that it blew up tyres, inside a minute, which was quite incredible for a man with fingers like pork sausages.

Jimmy gave his evidence about ordering me to get a haircut, and added one or two other little items for good measure. I then produced my star witness, the sergeant who saw me having my locks shorn on the previous evening.

After he marched out, there was a pregnant silence.

'Turn round,' Dolly Bear commanded.

I did so.

'I am going to alter this charge,' Dolly Bear said, 'to not having had an *adequate* haircut. I find the charge proved, and you will be reprimanded. March him out, sergeant-major!'

Later that day, Dolly Bear accosted me as I was passing his office.

'Ah, sergeant. I've changed my mind. I've decided to revert to the original charge, and remand you for the Officer Commanding tomorrow morning.'

Clearly Dolly Bear had discussed the situation with the OC, Major (Timber) Wood. Timber had obviously told him that it was unwise, even in the army, for a judge to change the nature of the charge in the middle of a trial, just because he couldn't make the original one stick. What if some beady-eyed lieutenant on the team of the Inspector-General at the next documentation check came across a copy of the 252, and decided to make an issue of it? Dolly Bear would be in for a chance of a swift posting, or at least a monumental bollocking, not to mention the Major as well, for having someone as thick as Dolly Bear under his command, and failing to do anything about it.

I went up before the major next morning. I was intrigued by his hair. It was a gingery-blond colour with a fast wave which favoured the left-hand side, and descended in a rippling cascade of curls to the nape of his neck, which combined with his pink complexion gave him something of the aspect of a Botticelli cherub – at least from behind.

Jimmy gave his evidence. My witness gave his.

Timber pondered for quite a long time, fingering the blue stubble on his chin. Eventually he said, 'Did you leave a lock of your hair on the sergeant-major's desk?'

'Before I answer that question sir,' I replied, 'perhaps you would be kind enough to inform me what it has to do with the charge on the charge sheet, which alleges that I failed to comply with the sergeant-major's order to get my hair cut.'

'Don't be impertinent, sergeant,' Timber said. 'I find the charge proved. You will receive a reprimand! March him out, sergeant-major.'

Timber was glad to see the back of me. He was terrified that I was going to demand a court-martial. I had no more haircut problems afterwards – about ten weeks later I had it cut voluntarily. It kept getting in my eyes.

OFFICERS

The real enemy!

The British Army's officers have traditionally emerged from the public school sector, which has always been considered the perfect training ground and launching pad for officer-like qualities – known as stiff upper lips. Nowadays, a fair proportion come from state schools but it has to be said that the main influence still comes from the public school tradition. Thus a cadet from South Reading Comprehensive who emerges from Sandhurst will, to all intents and purposes, appear almost indistinguishable from the products of Marlborough and Wellington.

The British system of class discrimination remains the most refined and sophisticated in the world. In civilian life there are infinite shades of grey. But in the services there is just black and white – the officers and the plebs. The system breaks down only at the 'sharp end'. If you are sharing a foxhole with an officer and scrap metal is whizzing around, you will quickly find yourself on Christian name terms.

Officers are sometimes – but not frequently – commissioned from the ranks, if only to support the old recruiting slogan, 'Every soldier carries a Field-Marshal's baton in his knapsack.' (Only one in history has ever held every rank.) The candidates are first of all put in front of a selection board of officers whose main concern is to find out whether they can tell a finger bowl from a fish finger.

The 'gentleman rankers' of Kipling's day – black sheep of noble familes – no longer exist. A young man with a public school accent and a double barrelled name who turned up at

a recruiting office, seeking to sign on as an ordinary squaddie, would be regarded with grave suspicion, given the address of the French Foreign Legion, and escorted out.

As in all other sections of the human species, there are good, and bad officers. The former should be cultivated, and kept sweet, the latter scrupulously avoided whenever possible. But confrontations with any officer should be circumvented. Even a good one can quickly turn barbary if he feels that his authority is being questioned.

There is a tradition of patriarchy in the British Army, a conviction among officers that they are acting *in parentis*, as father and mother to those under their command. Thus on a training exercise, the officers will see to it that the men are properly fed and watered before they sit down to their own repast. The real difference lies in the filling of the sandwiches – roast pork and pheasant, with whole grain mustard, as against cheese and corned beef.

The officers also concern themselves with the other ranks' body care. In the modern army most barracks are splendidly equipped with wash rooms, showers, etc. But it was not always so. I recall a camp in Scotland where some 200 other ranks had to share a bath house containing six baths. These baths had been installed about the time of the Crimean War, and were manufactured by Shanks & Co, a firm which had invented the cast iron bath during the early days of the Industrial Revolution. These examples were almost a century old and encrusted with the grime of several divisions of soldiery, most of them long dead. The splintered enamel

around the rims was mottled with rust and verdigris. After the first bath had been run, the temperature of the water emerging from both taps was strikingly similar – a little above freezing point. It was hardly surprising therefore that the bath house was not in constant use and, as a result, it was injudicious to stand down-wind when the whole company was on parade. For the first time the origin of the word 'ranker' was revealed.

When this lack of cleanliness came to the attention of the OC, Major Death (he pronounced it Dee-ath), he ordained that a bath rota should be kept. Every soldier was to have a bath once a week, and his attendance at the bath house duly recorded. The duty NCOs rapidly became rich from backhanders demanded for ticking off names on the roster, and the NAAFI did a roaring trade in pine scented talc.

The patriarchal attitude of officers also extends to social welfare. Other ranks who have domestic problems are encouraged to discuss them with their officer, and in some units one officer – normally a junior subaltern – is appointed to undertake the role normally assumed by social workers in civilian life. Thus you may arrive at a situation where a hairy forty-year-old gunner whose wife has just run off with a corporal in the redcaps, and who has a son in the Hell's Angels and a daughter in the pudding club, finds himself discussing these matters with a man twenty years younger, most of whose experience of life has been derived from a nanny and the housemaster of a boarding school.

But patriarchy can, and sometimes does, work both ways. I recall a general's inspection when I was serving as a sergeant in West Africa. It was a typically humid, sweaty sort of day. The whole company was paraded on the square in tropical kit and bush hats, glistening with perspiration after a brisk bout of marching up and down, and sideways. The general was due to arrive in five minutes. At this point the OC, a trim-moustached young major, emerged from his office and took over the parade from the sergeant-major. It was then that a grizzled old staff-sergeant, Dickie Brownlow, stepped out of the ranks, marched up to the major, exchanged a few words, turned about and marched back. The major also turned about and walked quickly back to his office. He reappeared shortly afterwards and took up his position just as the general's car cruised past the guard of honour at the main gate. Later, in the sergeants' mess, I asked Dickie what he had said to the major.

'I told him he'd got his hat on back to front.'

It has often been said that the British Army's NCOs comprise its backbone. The precise position of officers in its anatomy has yet to be positively identified, although various suggestions have been made. The much-quoted opinion by a German general in the First World War that the British Army was composed of 'lions led by donkeys' is unfortunately an assessment which still holds true today, though to be fair, mules would be a more accurate description. In my experience, the incomprehension of officers is nearly always compounded by a disposition towards obstinacy. They always *believe* they are right, against all the weight of evidence to the contrary.

Officers, like liquorice allsorts, come in a number of distinct varieties, and I will attempt in the following pages to describe one or two of the species. Yet whatever may be said about them – however perverse and exasperating their behaviour – it must always be remembered that they are, after all, trying.

GENERALS

In ordinary circumstances generals are too remote from the everyday activities of the average squaddie to pose any serious threat, apart from the nuisance value occasioned by the annual general's inspection. For about a week before this event the unit is at panic stations. Everything is spit and polished, scrubbed, painted, and drenched with water, or, if it moves, drilled and lectured and bollocked. Bullshit is rampant everywhere. Commanding Officers whose battalion is about to be inspected telephone the Commanding Officers of battalions which have recently been inspected, wanting to know what the general picked on . . . weapon training . . .? fire drill . . .? interior economy . . .? The generals know all about this, and pick on something different every time.

When the day comes every squaddie is paraded like a petrified penguin standing in his own puddle of water outside his place of employment, mugging up his lines. Inevitably – and almost certainly an hour behind schedule – the dreaded cohort appears, consisting of a red-tabbed general and general staff officer with green tabbed staff captain, accompanied by battalion CO, adjutant, and RSM.

You hope that they will pass you by with a cursory glance. But no . . . the general halts beside you, and fixes you with a beady stare.

'What would you do if you heard the fire alarm, corporal?'

'Erm . . . I'd shout "Fire", sir.'

'And what would you do when you'd shouted "Fire"?'

'Erm . . . erm . . . move quickly and quietly towards the source of the conflagration, sir.'

'I see.'

The general's lip curls with contempt. Your colonel screws up his eyes in pain. The RSM nods, grits his teeth, makes a mental note associated with the vengeance to come. The cohort moves on. You remain standing there, sweating with mortification which, after they are out of sight and you can stand down, gives way to defiance.

So what? You only got one bloody word wrong.

A squaddie's contact with generals is otherwise confined to marching past them at a saluting base, or listening to their speeches on occasions such as Armistice Day, or some sporting occasion like the Command Athletics Championships or the Corps Shoot at Bisley. Whenever a general makes a speech at such an event, the weather is always inclement. He will be standing on a heap of duckboards in the pissing rain, while a second-lieutenant holds a red and yellow-striped umbrella over his head. A blustery wind will be tearing loudly at the flaps of the adjacent tents. The amplification equipment will utter a piercing screech every fifteen seconds and the general's delivery, muffled at the point of exit by his Kitchener moustache and thereafter buffeted this way and that by the gale force blast, is only to be picked up in dribs and drabs.

'. . . first class sporting spirit . . . Duke of Wellington once said . . . benign providence . . . individual performance . . . working as a team . . . healthy antagonism . . . the battlefield of life . . . if only our Russian friends . . . always ask my wife . . . shake hands like a . . . young subaltern serving in India at the time . . . wise advice I'd like to pass on . . . if God had to make a choice between . . .'

The masses watch the colonel who lurks at the general's shoulder. When he guffaws at the delivery of a punch line they bare their teeth and some of the bravest cackle or neigh. The speech ends. The colonel whisks off his cap and holds it high.

'Three cheers for General Sir Alistair Macallister. Hip hip . . .'

'Hooray!'
'Hip hip . . .'
'Hooray!'
'Hip hip . . .'
'Hooray!'
The general tugs at his cap and climbs quickly into his waiting car.

Ordeal over!

The bar is open. There is a sudden stampede across the bruised and sodden turf towards the distant marquee.

Every soldier has the right to a personal interview with his general. It's one means of becoming famous throughout the battalion, but can sometimes be a serious tactical mistake.

First of all, the reasons for the interview must be written down and presented to the Commanding Officer.

'Ah, Hopkins, I understand from this application that you feel your company sergeant-major has been picking on you unfairly.'

'Yes sir.'

'Well, this is a matter which we can sort out within the battalion. There's no need for you to see the general. Now ahm . . .'

'I'd rather see the general sir, if you don't mind.'

'I see. Hmmmmm!'

The general will give you fifteen seconds of his time, during which he will do all the talking. He will explain that your complaint is an internal matter for the unit, and he is referring it back to your Commanding Officer.

After that you slap in for a posting, and pray that it comes through soon.

*

The closest I got to a general happened when I was posted to Lagos. After a few weeks of the military social life – twice-weekly bingo sessions in the sergeants' mess – I joined a club in the town whose membership was largely African with a smattering of British expatriates. It wasn't long before I met Ade, editor of the *Daily Service,* a Nigerian national newspaper. Thereafter I contributed a weekly column under the pseudonym 'Cyclops', where I discoursed upon the social and political issues of the day.

Nigeria, at the time, was involved in the final independence negotiations with the then Prime Minister, Sir Anthony Eden. I was particularly severe on Eden, who appeared to me to be dragging his feet. (He justified my distrust soon afterwards by trying to start the Third World War over the Suez Canal business.)

42

There was a buzz of speculation around the administration concerning the identity of 'Cyclops'. One Saturday I attended a Derby Day function at the club, where we joined together with the members of another club which was largely expatriate British with a smattering of Africans. Over wine and sandwiches we listened to the race on the radio from England and placed our bets with a local bookie. I was introduced to a fellow-guest in a linen jacket who looked as if he had just walked out of an old Bulldog Drummond movie.

'I'd like you to meet General Willoughby.'

I realised that I was confronting the GOC, West Africa Command. We shook hands briskly.

'Ah . . . I understand you're the chap who writes the Cyclops column?'

'Erm . . . excuse me . . . I'll just go and refresh my glass.'

I wandered off and sneaked out through a side door.

I saw the general once more, about six weeks later. He was paying a routine visit to my unit, and had dropped into the sergeants' mess for the statutory formal drink. We lined up in our monkey jackets and cummerbunds. The RSM introduced us. As he approached I thrust out my chin and tried to do something Chinese with my eyes – anything to look different. I needn't have bothered. He nodded affably and passed on – I noticed that his own eyes were glazed with boredom. Mine was just another face in a hundred thousand, in sergeants' messes all over the world.

ADJUTANTS

Whenever there is a vacancy for an adjutant in a battalion, the Commanding Officer will select a captain who has the best qualifications to fill this role. These are self-importance, total insensitivity, and a congenital dislike and distrust of his own species. He will not be difficult to identify. He will sport a bristly little moustache, have eyes like black-currants within spitting distance of each other, and finely chiselled nostrils which dilate and deflate continuously. And he always carries a silver-knobbed stick, which he slaps gently against his thighs, except when he taps it against the chest of some unfortunate recruit.

'You – what's your name?'

'Chadwick, sir.'

'Chadwick, eh? Good. What's the first objective of an infantry soldier, Chadwick?'

'Kill the enemy, sir.'

'Good . . . good. How often do you wash your hair, Chadwick?'

'Twice a week, sir.'

'Well, it doesn't look like it to me!'

The adjutant will also take it upon himself to dampen the spirits of exuberant young subalterns.

'Ah, Mr Prothero . . . you're rather partial to Gevrey Chambertin, I gather.'

'Well, it is a bit more-ish, sir, wouldn't you say?'

'Oh, quite. As a matter of fact Colonel Saxelby was entertaining the GSO to dinner last night and he was asking for a bottle . . . but it would appear that you and your friend Mr Briggs have managed to guzzle our entire stock.'

'Oh no . . . Oh my God . . . look, I'm most awfully sorry.'

Adjutants spend much of their time composing items for the Daily Regimental Orders designed to clamp down on the convenience and pleasures of subordinates.

'Other ranks will not play football, or indulge in any other activity during off-duty hours, in the main car park, which is reserved exclusively for the parking of cars.'

'After any social event in the other ranks' canteen, all female

guests must be escorted off the camp premises by 2300 hours.'

'Under no circumstances will other ranks be permitted to make or receive private telephone calls on military telephones, unless in emergency situations such as the death of a close relative, and then only with the written permission of the Commanding Officer.'

'All personnel are warned that the defacing of lavatory walls by graffiti must cease immediately. Unless this instruction is rigidly observed, the doors of all lavatories in other ranks' quarters will be removed.'

From the other ranks' point of view adjutants are not so much to be feared as their equally obnoxious acolytes, the RSMs (see under Regimental Sergeant-Majors), since they are rather less in evidence, and a good many of their snappy little instructions can be outflanked or undermined. I once received a note from one of them, passed on (with interest) from the RSM, which stated, 'Sergeant Holles will not smoke his pipe when cycling past the CO's office.' On future occasions when I was pedalling past the CO's office I would steer the bike with one hand, while ostentatiously removing the pipe and holding it an inch in front of my teeth.

The only time I had a real problem with an adjutant was when I was attached as armourer sergeant to an infantry battalion in Wiltshire. I never discovered why this one should have singled me out – perhaps he observed me cycling around the camp in an insolent manner with my belt on upside down – but he stomped into my workshop one afternoon with his dog, a paunchy bull terrier, waddling at his heels.

He waggled his stick furiously.

'This place is like a slum . . . it's absolutely disgusting! Look at all that filth under the bench.'

I respectfully pointed out that the filth under the bench consisted of wood shavings which would be swept up at the end of the day's work.

'Those windows,' he fulminated. 'When were they last cleaned?' He ran his finger along the sill and held it up for my inspection. 'Look at that!'

The pooch muttered and grumbled deep inside its throat. A thin trickle of saliva drooled from its jowl and formed glistening bobbles on the floor.

'You will have this place spotlessly clean by 1100 hours tomorrow,' snarled its master, 'when it will be inspected by the RSM.'

He tucked his stick under his armpit and stomped out. The cur gave me a sidelong glance of cold contempt and followed.

The RSM duly inspected at the appointed hour. I had swamped everything – floor, benches, windows – with water. (In the army, when anything is seen to be wet, it is presumed to be clean.) As he left, he informed me that I had been nominated commander of the town picquet on the following Saturday night.

This information was rather disquieting as I had made other arrangements for that particular evening. Furthermore, attached personnel such as myself were supposed to be excused all regimental duties – it said so in Queen's Regulations. I looked up the appropriate section and asked for an interview with my company commander.

It was, on reflection, an error of judgement. When I outlined my case, giving it chapter and verse, the major stiffened and gripped the edge of his desk.

'Are you trying to instruct me in Queen's Regulations, sergeant?'

'Oh no, sir . . . that wasn't my intention at all. I was simply trying to explain that . . .'

'Get out!'

The adjutant had clearly got to him first.

On the following Saturday at 2100 hours, I commenced my duties as commander of the town picquet in Warminster. For the next three hours I was due to patrol the streets with a squad of four men, in the interests of military discipline. Warminster was a small garrison town and on a Saturday night it was crowded with the assorted soldiery of various units, hunting for crumpet in the streets and dance halls, or getting cheerfully smashed in the local pubs. It was my province to seek out the preternaturally stroppy and the fighting drunk, from those who were merely improperly dressed, and give them a bad time. We duly emerged from the garrison guardroom, clutching our pickaxe handles, and marched off in single file to the town.

It was one of the few occasions when I was favoured by fortune. I'd got married a few weeks earlier and had just installed myself, with wife, in a rented flat which just happened to be located in Warminster High Street. I marched the squad up to the front door, and opened i.. We all filed in.

For most of the next three hours we sat drinking light ale, eating my wife's home-made sausage rolls, and listening to *Saturday Night Theatre* on the radio. Just before midnight I announced, 'Right, there's another ten minutes before we go off-duty. We'd better have a stroll up the street and back, just to show our faces.' Two of the squad went on ahead – they returned a minute or so later, pallid as chalk in the artificial glow of the street lights.

'The Cameronians are having a punch up with the Leicesters just outside the Wagon and Horses,' one of them told me. 'There's all sorts of blood and snot flying about.'

I looked at my watch.

'We've just got time,' I said, 'to see what's going on in the Town Hall area.'

When I checked out at midnight I was obliged to sign the Incident Book. In the appropriate space I wrote 'None'.

I was never selected for town picquet duty again.

QUARTERMASTERS

Some soldiers have the very laudable ambition of finding themselves a cushy billet in the stores. There is good sense in this, not least because storemen are excused most parades and several other equally noxious duties. While their comrades are slogging through the pounding rain on night marches, they will be snuggled up in their pits. But before you take an irretrievable step, it is always useful to do some research into the character and personality of the resident Quartermaster. If he is a decent bloke, you'll be quids in. On the other hand, if he happens to be a pig's orphan (which is not unusual), he will make your life hell on legs.

*

Quartermasters are a special breed of officer appointed to units of battalion strength to run the stores, services, and accommodation. They are drawn exclusively from the ranks and most of them have some twenty years of service behind them and have already achieved the rank of RSM or Regimental Quartermaster-Sergeant. Since they are too set in their ways to adapt to the normal officer pattern, they tend to stand out like teazles in a bunch of lilies.

One example I recall was Ben, formerly an RSM, a bulky man with features like a green pepper beginning to ripen. He had become well known for various eccentricities, such as turning out to referee a battalion rugger match on a Sunday afternoon, stoned out of his mind. When he was commissioned, the CO apportioned him a small annexe in the officers' mess where he could take his meals in private.

Ben considered this a privilege accorded to him in recognition of his seniority. The real reason was that the other officers couldn't bear to listen to him eat.

Another prize example was Freddy – also a former RSM – whose complexion was that of oatmeal porridge, garnished by a hog's bristle moustache. Freddy appeared to consider that the apportioning of stores and equipment was in his personal gift. At the weekly sessions when the company quartermaster-sergeants brought in their items for clothing exchange, Freddy would contemptuously pick up a boot with the sole hanging from the uppers and toss it back on the heap.

'Get these round to the cobbler's shop,' he would snarl. 'There's another two years' life in 'em.' And similarly he would go through the sad heaps of threadbare clothing. 'Haven't your people ever heard of a needle and cotton?'.

Freddy would then go into a furious bollocking routine, at which he was a master. His icy-blue eyes would bulge with outrage. A scarlet flush would creep up his neck. His voice would rise to a paranoic scream. Who did they think he was? Freeman Hardy and bloody Willis? How dared they waste his time?

A bollocking from Freddy was a truly traumatic experience, so frightening that it produced a surge of hysteria in the victim, an insane desire to laugh which had to be rigorously suppressed. One came away from it sweating cogs, blinking gratefully into the sunlight, gulping in the fresh air. One of the quartermaster-sergeants refused to go anywhere near him after his first such encounter. His company gradually came to resemble a band of ragged-arsed mercenaries.

As I was on Freddy's staff, I received the full treatment more than once. Yet eventually he was to provide one of my life's intense moments of pleasure. It was on a troopship coming back from Korea.

A few words about troopships. They have become almost redundant now, most troops being transported overseas by air. From the other ranks' point of view this is an important advance. Troopships were never places for rest and relaxation. Military authority has always held that they were dangerous breeding grounds for unrest, even mutiny, among the sweaty denizens of the troopdecks. The other ranks had to be kept constantly on the move with PT sessions, kit inspections, herded hither and thither to tedious little lectures by medical officers (graphically illustrated), concerning the dangers of picking up a full house from tropical whores. Morale was not helped by daily doses of bromide in the tea, designed to quash any lecherous ambitions towards the handful of nurses in the 'A' deck cabins. (They were strictly for the officers.)

A special squad of NCOs – usually selected from Correction Centre screws who needed a change of scenery – were responsible for discipline among the troops in transit. Every four or five minutes a rasping voice would emerge from the public address system:

'Private Banks will report to the troopdeck – NOW!'

The unfortunate nominee would have been spotted flicking a dog-end through a porthole, or found responsible for having the edge of a jockstrap poking out from his neatly-folded blankets. He would be given a harsh and rancorous wigging and punished with a three-day spell of duty cleaning rifles in some dark hole some eight or nine decks down.

I was surprised to notice that Freddy, when I came across him from time to time, seemed quite at ease with himself. He could be seen chatting affably to other officers – sometimes he would even toss a jocular remark to a passing corporal. Perhaps he was just glad to be going home, but I suspected another reason. The whole atmosphere of the ship seethed and crackled with furious bollockings. Freddy could afford to relax. Others were doing his work for him.

As we churned through the Bay of Biscay there was another in the frequent succession of lifeboat drills. Everyone had to pick up a lifejacket, put it on, and parade in a pre-ordained position on the lifeboat deck. The life jackets were stored in lockers all over the ship. You were told exactly which locker to go to, and many of them were some distance away from the troopdecks and cabins.

Freddy, resenting this rude incursion into his new-found peace, grabbed a lifejacket from the nearest locker and ambled up on deck for the inspection. This was carried out by a small gaggle of officers headed by the ship's CO, a Lieutenant-Colonel in a Highland regiment. He was a man of some six and a half feet and eighteen stone, wearing a kilt and glengarry. A network of purple veins spread from the base of his nose across his formidable jowls – he must have been weaned on neat Chivas Regal.

Standing a few yards from Freddy, I watched this little cohort approach. They halted some fifteen yards away, and I heard a corporal being screamed at for not wearing a life jacket. He maintained that when he went to the locker to collect it, the locker was empty. The file moved slowly on until it reached Freddy. A junior officer looked at the reference number stamped on his lifejacket. It bore the wrong code. This was brought to the attention of the colonel. He peered at Freddy for a few moments as if inspecting an insect. His jowls quivered. Then he launched himself into the most monumental bollocking I had ever heard.

Was Freddy aware that because of his idleness and selfishness in taking a lifejacket from the wrong locker he had put the life of another soldier at risk? Did he have the impertinence to call himself an officer and a gentleman? Or did he consider himself above and beyond the ship's safety regulations? In forty years of service, at home and abroad, the colonel had never encountered such disgraceful behaviour . . .

It was not a strong voice, emerging as it did from so large and powerful a frame. The delivery was a ferocious, high-pitched, nagging whine, like a hornet trapped in a shoe-box. But it was deeply etched with a withering contempt and it went on for rather a long time. Even from ten yards distance I found it almost unbearable to listen to. After a while, everyone in the vicinity began to fidget and shuffle their feet, longing for the colonel to stop. It was more than mortal men could stand.

Freddy seemed riveted to the deck. His features gradually assumed the pallor of a corpse. Beads of sweat began to pimple his forehead. Mercifully, the colonel reached the end of his peroration before Freddy started foaming at the mouth. The colonel ordered him to hand his lifejacket to the corporal with an apology, and to parade outside his (the colonel's) office an hour later wearing the correct one.

It would not be true to say that Freddy never administered another bollocking in his life. But somehow the sting went out of them, they were almost friendly, he could no longer summon up the bile which had made them so exceptional in the past.

So much for officers. Let us now consider the remainder of the opposition – warrant officers and NCOs.

REGIMENTAL SERGEANT-MAJORS

In units of battalion strength, the Adjutant is responsible for discipline, the RSM for its implementation. His province is that of the major-domo, the eyes and ears of the Commanding Officer, a roaring, self-important *prima donna* who is supposed to keep the other ranks 'on their toes'. The effect is generally to create an atmosphere of gloom and fear – there is a strong case for the abolition of RSMs in the interests of morale.

I have encountered a few decent ones, but by and large, Regimental Sergeant-Majors represent the very epitome of indoctrination, the complete end-product of the military ideal. Anyone who has ever served as a ranker in the army will recall a prize specimen or two of his own. There was, for example, Splitpin Edmonds, whose legs appeared to reach all the way up to his armpits as he bestrode the parade grounds of Catterick like a poisonous stick insect.

There was also 'Helmut' Knaggs – two hundred pounds of cold pork and streaky bacon, with piggy little eyes and a voice like a donkey with asthma. He was about as welcome around the barracks as Mrs Thatcher would be if she turned up at the Durham Miners' Gala.

Least loved of all, perhaps was 'Turk' Taylor, who once infested the barrack squares of Arborfield. He stood five feet seven, and the soles of his boots were as thick as wedding cakes to compensate for his lack of inches. He could turn bright crimson in a matter of seconds when delivering a bollocking, and his rancour was always reserved for men larger than himself – which included nearly everyone. The bigger they were, the harder they had to fall. He would have a man of six feet four double marking time while he remorselessly cut him down to size for some monstrous breach of discipline such as scratching his nose during the playing of the national anthem.

Most RSMs, down the years, have developed a stock of witty repartee, such as:

'I've seen jelly babies do it better!'

'Don't move until I tell you, Hutchins . . . because I'm standing on your hair!'

'I can't imagine why you joined the army, lad. You could 'ave made a fortune makin' television commercials for Brooke Bond bloody tea bags.'

'Have you got a double, Parsons?'

'No sir, not to my knowledge.'

'Well, you have now, lad . . . you've gotta double round the square for bein' idle. Go on . . . move!'

'If you don't smarten yourself up, laddie, I'm going to have to put you on the list of endangered species!'

'I never believed there was such a thing as a male meno-pause until I came across you lot. Wake your ideas up!'

The way to survive this constant barrage of insult is to think of apt rejoinders (which of course are never actually delivered).

'Er . . . excuse me sir. What would an ignorant pisshead like you know about the nature of ideas, since you've obvi-ously never had one you could call your own?'

or

'Sir, I've been given to understand that they're starting up a rest home on the outskirts of Aldershot for ageing fascist baboons. I wonder if you'd like me to put you on the waiting list?'

or

'If you will insist on spraying my handsome features with your revolting spittle, you bastard, you might at least have the decency to refrain from eating pickled onions first!'

The RSM also runs the Sergeants' Mess, and presides at

58

the monthly mess meetings. I recall one addressing the assembled WOs and Sergeants in the following terms:

'Last month we had a dance and social evenin' in the mess. There were at least a dozen members absent. Right. We've got another social evenin' comin' up on Saturday week. Every member of this mess will attend unless he is excused by me personally – and he'll need to have a bloody good reason. And all those members livin' in married quarters will be accompanied by their wives. Is that clear?'

Most RSMs, however, like to feel that there is another side to their nature – a kindly, compassionate, almost sentimental streak. I once observed the features of one crack into a snaggle-toothed smile as he listened to a fragment of Gilbert and Sullivan played by the Regimental Band . . . the first stirring, perhaps, of cultural awareness. Another, at a transit camp where I was incarcerated for a few weeks awaiting a posting, took me aside.

'I understand you're a bit of a writer,' he said gruffly.

I had recently published my first book. Word had clearly got around to strange places.

'Er, yes sir, I do a bit from time to time.'

'You writing anything now?'

'No, not really.'

'Why not?'

'Well, you see sir, you need a bit of privacy to write. Otherwise it's difficult to concentrate.'

'Right, I'll see what I can do.'

On the following day he sent for me. 'I've found you a separate room where you can write away to your heart's content,' he said. 'Come on, I'll show you where it is.'

The room he showed me was the annexe to the blanco room. I was soon installed there with a trestle table, a chair, an old Underwood typewriter, and a hundred sheets of blank paper. All through the day soldiers would tramp in and out to blanco their equipment in the room beyond. They would peer over my shoulder. 'What you writin' about then, sarge?' Every day the RSM asked me if I had finished something for him to read. By the time my posting arrived I was becoming paranoid.

But perhaps the most petrifying encounter I had with a member of this species was when I was stationed at the Tower of London, and the nagging insistence of a decaying wisdom tooth forced me to visit the District Dental Officer, who happened to have his surgery at Chelsea Barracks. The subsequent extraction required the application of anaesthetic gas. I vaguely recall spitting into a pan, stumbling out of the torture chamber, along a long brown corridor, down some flights of stone steps, and emerging into a welcome sunlit space.

Suddenly the mist in my head cleared. I was standing in the middle of a parade ground in my greasy denim overalls, my sergeants' stripes hanging to my arm by a single brass split pin. I was bareheaded, having left my beret in the dentist's waiting room. Some fifteen yards to my left a squad of about sixty Grenadier Guards in red coats and bearskins were paraded in the 'present arms' position with fixed bayonets.

I rapidly became fully conscious, and glanced to my right. I saw a Guards' Adjutant mounted on a big piebald stallion. Next to him – some three yards away from me – was a Guards Regimental Sergeant-Major in full regalia.

There was an eerie silence. I saw the RSM's jaw drop in blank astonishment, revealing the saliva glistening on the pork-choppy mucous membrane, studded with the black and silver mementoes of past dentistry performed, perhaps, by the monster two storeys up in the block behind.

The stallion, first to catch the whiff of incipient panic, scraped its forefeet, gave a shrill whinny, accompanied by a crisp fart. I glanced around. On one side, the uninviting façade of the barrack block. On two others, acres of grey tarmac. On the fourth side, some thirty yards distant, the high brick perimeter wall and the massive, closed, wrought-iron gates. But inside one of them a small, man-sized wicket-door which mercifully hung open.

I was through it in perhaps three seconds and careering past the startled window shoppers among the boutiques of the King's Road. I had reached Sloane Square before I heard the echo of a distant scream rattle across the façade of the Royal Court Theatre. 'Staaaaaaaaa . . . aand still!'

The placards announced a new play – *Look Back in Anger*.

NON-COMMISSIONED OFFICERS

The dishing out of rank with identifiable badges is one of the oldest con-tricks in the world – it was already thousands of years old before the stick-and-carrot technique was invented (by Good King Wenceslaus). The idea – a brilliant one – was that the best way of controlling the plebs was by appointing some of them to exercise authority over the others. This having been accomplished, the aristos could relax and concentrate on the more serious issues such as wining, dining and wenching, with a little hunting for exercise.

The system is firmly rooted in basic human psychology. Once you've got two tapes you feel infinitely superior to somebody who's only got one, and you can't wait until you've got three.

It's much the same thing with campaign ribbons. If you see a squaddie with two or three up – and they're always designed in bright colours so that they can't be ignored – you're supposed to be impressed. Here's a bloke who's been somewhere and done something. But the chances are he acquired them by going to some high risk area and doing what he was told when he got there. It's much more impressive if a bloke's got ten years' service in and not a single ribbon to show for it on his chest – there stands a man who's mastered the art of keeping out of trouble.

The Chinese Army abolished rank altogether in the recent past and everyone took turns to lead the platoon. But results during the Korean War, and that rather messy little contretemps with the North Vietnamese, didn't quite come up to expectations, so they've now started sprouting stars and stripes again.

A bit of rank, however, is always useful. When you haven't got any, you're at the mercy of about half the British Army. When you get as far as sergeant, you're only at the mercy of about a quarter of it. Moreover you've got a bit of privacy, a reasonable salary (provided you're not too ambitious, and don't play the horses), and if you can manage to maintain a low profile, your life style can be modestly enjoyable.

The first stage on your way up – the dogleg – is perhaps the most difficult. It is the occasion when you leave the cheerful camaraderie of the formidable mass of the stripeless and join the ranks of the enemy, but without any real status or authority.

Lance-corporals are a bit of a joke, despised by those beneath and exploited by those above; they are given nasty little duties like hanging around the hotplate in the dining hall at noshing time, studying all the faces in the queue, and attempting to stop anyone from coming round for a second helping of cod and chips.

'All right Charlie, let's stop being too bloody greedy, eh? You're carrying a sight too much freight in front there as it is. All right then . . . but just this once, mind.'

A lance-corporal is appointed – and frequently dis-appointed – at the whim of the Commanding Officer. I once knew a soldier called 'Gary' Cooper, who had held the rank, over some forty years of service, eleven times, and been busted as many. At the time I first knew him, he had just been busted once again. On this occasion, he'd been commander of the squad guarding the silver at the Regimental Ball. Late in the evening he'd been caught taking a quiet piss into a tub of pot plants by the Brigadier's wife.

However, the gaining of the first stripe is an all-important step in the pursuit of comfort and requires a little care and concentration. It is essential, for a start, to go for at least six months without being on a fizzer, and one should not be ashamed of doing a bit of creeping (of which more later), especially around officers:

'Oh er, excuse me sir, I just happened to see your 1926 Bugatti in the officers' car park . . . it's a marvellous old piece of machinery, isn't it, sir. If you ever want someone to give it a lick of polish sometime I'd be only too . . .'

'Oh no, sir, I certainly wouldn't want paying for it, I mean it would be a kind of labour of love if you know what I mean . . . I've always been fascinated by . . .'

('*A couple of quid? Up your arse, Captain Fernyhough, you pompous little tightwad . . .*')

'Oh, right, sir. I'll nip over tomorrow evening . . . oh and I think we'll need some of that special silver polish for the headlamps . . . what do they call it? Silvicrene I think.'

The rank of full corporal embodies a certain degree of

security. Since it's a full rank it can't be taken away arbitrarily by the CO if you happen to get up his nose. If you unwisely stray too far off course, he can fit you up with a court martial and have you stripped that way, but there's always a risk that you might hire yourself a smart lawyer and get away with it. So it's much more likely that he'll take the easy way out and have you posted to somewhere like South Armagh, or St Kilda, where you'll commune with the sheep and the seagulls, in the teeth of a freezing gale.

But full corporals have to be carefully watched from the viewpoint of those on the receiving end – real indoctrination starts here. If your man is young and eager and sweating on his third, he could be a real problem, snarling and yapping like a Queen's corgi, and tearing off charge sheets like toilet paper in a hospital for tropical diseases.

Sergeants tend to be a more relaxed breed – apart from those who are sweating on accelerated promotion by making life a misery for the bodies below. As a general rule, they are placed on a regimental promotion list and have to wait for dead mens' boots before they get their crown up, by which time most of them are cheerfully grafting away in civvy street. The third tape also guarantees entry to the Sergeants' Mess, which can be quite an agreeable club, always provided that the RSM isn't some roaring manic depressive who is always 'on parade'.

SALUTING

This is the archaic practice of a soldier throwing up his right hand to the peak of his cap whenever he encounters an officer. The officer, in response, will crook a finger in the vague direction of his ear. The custom derives from the Middle Ages when serfs were obliged to touch their forelocks to the squire and other gentry. (Those who declined could be found discussing their grievances together in the local workhouse.)

Some wise and experienced officers aren't too fussy about the saluting business. Those who have to be watched are the second lieutenants fresh out of Sandhurst, and women officers up to the rank of major-general. (Or whatever the female equivalent is.)

Since saluting can be a rather demeaning affair, especially in the case of an officer for whom one has little or no affection, it needs to be avoided whenever possible. Sometimes the sting can be removed by giving your ear a quick scratch before putting your hand down, as if this was the primary purpose of the exercise.

Buildings are always useful. When you see an officer approaching in an area where buildings are present, you simply turn off and go through the nearest door, emerging when the officer has passed. If the door won't open, you can either knock on it, or pretend to be searching your pockets for the key.

Every soldier should develop a defensive technique in case he is caught in the open – perhaps feigning preoccupation with his private thoughts so that he will not even notice a passing officer. The ensuing dialogue goes something like this:

'I say, come back here, that man!'

'Sir?'

'Are you in the habit of not saluting officers?'

'No, sir.'

'Then why didn't you salute me?'

'Well sir, I was just coming across the football field when I happened to fall over on a patch of slippery grass. I think I've put my shoulder out, sir.'

'Well in that case, why didn't you give me an "eyes right"?'

'I think I've ricked my neck as well, sir. I'm just going down to the MI room to see if I can get some treatment.'

Soon after I was demobilised I wrote to the Ministry of

Defence suggesting that this primitive practice should now be abandoned. I pointed out that assuming a salute lasts about five seconds and that the average soldier delivers half a dozen a day, then throughout the combined services in the course of a year, some half a million man hours are expended by men throwing their arms up at each other. Perhaps this time could be spent more profitably.

I am still waiting for a reply.

CEREMONIAL

This is a component of military life which should be avoided wherever possible. There is nothing more tedious than pounding up a High Street behind a band, then having to stand for an hour in a vicious north-easterly, while assorted nonentities such as the Deputy Assistant Secretary to the Ministry of Defence make boring speeches.

One well-tried tactic is to develop a malfunction of the feet and get oneself excused boots – permanently. Success here, however, usually depends on the availability of a young and gullible medical officer, or a clerk in the orderly room who is willing to provide the necessary documentation, complete with forged signature, for the usual consideration.

It's also a good idea to arrange for a period of leave to coincide with 11 November. This is always a gala day for ceremonial parades, and nearly always an unspeakably wet one, too. (The purgatory continues with a second course consisting of sitting in a freezing cathedral listening to some bishop droning on.)

There is one weakness in the system which is capable of exploitation. Since the parade is a public spectacle, the sergeant-major in charge of it will be anxious about his reputation – he will become paranoid in advance about any sloppiness in front of the War Memorial, and thus will tend to select his squad with care. A soldier with the right attitude will make sure he is not among the chosen few. If, however, by some mistake he finds himself in the squad, a reasonable amount of cack-handedness with the hardware during the rehearsals (such as dropping it), will probably ensure his

71

swift replacement. He will not be excused entirely but probably given some menial task such as dishing out the hymn sheets – although here there is always an even chance of slipping into the local boozer for half an hour while the wreaths are being laid.

If all such ruses fail, however, and one finds oneself strapped into a greatcoat, porting a bondick, and trudging behind a band, the best way to take one's mind off the attendant boredom and misery is to formulate words to the martial music. The libretto of some of the popular favourites such as 'Colonel Bogey' is well enough known to every soldier, as are the words to Sousa's 'National Emblem'. (Have you ever caught your bollocks in a rat trap?) Another familiar refrain is the one which runs, 'Twenty-one, never been done, Queen of all the Fairies . . . ain't it a pity she's only one titty to feed the baby on . . .'

The marches of Kenneth Alford are particularly suited to the verbal treatment. For instance:

Cap . . . tains are ever so nice . . .
Ma . . . jors are sticky with lice . . .
Colonels are stern bulls . . .
And Brigadiers are thick as dear old mice.
(To tune of 'The Thin Red Line')

Sergeant-majors have always been well-represented:

Our Sergeant-major's got a crown upon 'is arm . . .
Our Sergeant-major's got a crown upon 'is arm . . .
Our Sergeant-major's got a crown upon 'is arm . . .
But 'e thinks 'e's got it on 'is bleedin' 'ead.
(To tune of 'John Brown's Body')

There's another march, the title of which escapes me, the first line of which runs: 'How can I draw rations . . . when I haven't got a chit?' The rest of the refrain is too offensive to the military hierarchy to be reproduced here.

*

Since my own limitations on the parade ground were recognised at an early stage, I had few problems in the ceremonial stakes – I was not fit to be put before the general public, and that was that. But I did have one minor setback during my service which occurred when an unfortunate colleague handed in his checks prematurely. It was decided from on high that the funeral party would consist of every sergeant in the unit.

Rehearsals began immediately. They involved rather complicated exercises such as swivelling one's rifle until it was upside down, and then leaning on it in a sort of attitude of prayer. After the second rehearsal the sergeant-major accepted that I was unlikely to master this technique in the allotted time-span – if ever – and I was stood down. But I was delegated to accompany the funeral party and given a specific task. When they came to the point where they were required to remove head-dress, I was to move quietly along the file and collect their berets. I did so most assiduously. The earth was scattered, the volley fired over the coffin. It was time to move off. I walked smartly along the front of the file, handing back the headgear. Unfortunately, I started at the wrong end. As the funeral party marched sombrely away, it was noticeable that some berets were perched on top like peas upon a drum, others drooped over the eyelids.

The only other occasion I got involved in military ceremonial was when I was posted to the Tower of London, and my participation was entirely involuntary. I was given a small cell in the main barrack block, which was built into the works of a gigantic clock which whirred and whizzed and grunted the whole time, except every fifteen minutes when it would boom and clang with a force which made the walls vibrate. After the first few sleepless nights I decided to wander out one evening and get agreeably stewed in the neighbouring Whitechapel pubs. Perhaps it would cure my insomnia.

It was early December. When I returned to the Tower just before eleven, a thick bank of fog had rolled up from the

Thames and settled over the bleak escarpments like a blanket of porridge. Visibility was about a yard. As the gatekeeper let me in, he mumbled what I thought was an unintelligible oath. (I realised later it was the password.) As I stumbled across the cobbles towards Traitors' Gate, I suddenly heard a scream of 'Halt! Who goes there?' very close to my left eardrum. I made out the crouching figure of a sentry of the Welsh Guards, replete with rifle and fixed bayonet. But he was facing away from me.

Another voice came rumbling out of the murk.

'The Keys!'

'Whose Keys?' bellowed the sentry.

'The Queen's Keys!' snarled the other voice.

I kept moving, and bumped into the rotund figure of a beefeater who was holding out a silk cushion. On it was the biggest bunch of keys I'd ever seen. As we collided he tottered and the keys nearly slid off, but he managed to keep them on by a nifty piece of footwork.

'Pass on, the Queen's Keys. All's Well!' the sentry hollered.

Peering through the misty gloom, I identified the portly outlines of six other beefeaters flanking the one with the cushion. Recognising that a difficult situation might be about to materialise, I elected to evacuate the location smartly but I suddenly found myself blundering about among another couple of tons of unyielding flesh – an escort party of guardsmen, all wearing rifles with fixed bayonets.

I recall knocking one or two off balance as I thrashed about. I stuck my flailing fingers into a bulging neck, heard some harsh cursing very close to my lobe, and then I was through them and away like the ghost of the Earl of Essex. It took me another half an hour to grope my way back to my billet, nearly walking into the river twice, and three times having to melt into solid granite when challenged by a sentry. Soon after I bolted the door behind me the clock struck midnight. The racket was indescribable but this time it was almost comforting.

SPORT

There is an alleged tradition in the army that 'there is no rank on the field of play'.

Forget it!

I have never known a battalion rugby team, containing the usual complement of about ten officers, where the skipper is a corporal. On the other hand I've played rugger against a guards' battalion where the skipper – a major – dished out the instructions as if he was on parade, and the other rank element sprang to attention and clicked their heels together in response.

When young and fit, I used to play rugby for a Home Counties team, Marlow, where I flourished as a centre three-quarter, having a yard or two of pace, a few extra pounds for bullocking through the middle, and a crafty side-step. When I turned out for the battalion, however, I was forced to play on the wing, since the two centre spots were allocated to a major, and a captain.

I played outside the captain, and had plenty of time to observe his technique. He always needed to be standing still when he received the ball, and invariably got an opponent simultaneously. Whenever the ball was in play elsewhere, he would stand crouching forward, as if eager to get off the mark, and would frequently turn to me, wagging a hand.

'Up a bit, corporal,' he would shout. Or, 'Back a bit, corporal.'

Eventually frustration overcame prudence. I hollered back, 'What's the point of saying up a bit corporal and back a bit, corporal – I never get the bloody ball!'

Other ranks who enjoy their sport should stay away, if possible, from those dominated by officers, such as rugby, golf, squash, tennis, and – in particular – cricket. I recall an occasion at Colchester where a young subaltern was posted to the battalion. In order to ingratiate himself with his company commander, who was also skipper of the cricket team, he announced that he was a keen cricketer.

'Oh, really?'

'Yes I er . . . turned out regularly at school. Of course I'm a little rusty.'

'Bat or bowl?'

'Bit of both, actually.'

'Care for a game next Saturday?'

'Yes I think I would, rather.'

On the day of the match twelve players turned up to play for the battalion. Eleven were officers, the twelfth a raw-boned lance-corporal who normally opened the bowling.

'Oh er . . . Corporal Grimsby. We appear to be one too many. I wonder if you'd like to do the scoring?'

'Sir!'

The subaltern got a duck and twenty-seven runs came from his single over.

I was never a good cricketer myself, but I've always enjoyed the game, and once, as a lance-corporal at Bordon, I wandered down to the sports field one Saturday afternoon to watch a game in progress. The skipper of our team was the battalion CO, Lieut-Col. Rotton. (He pronounced it Row-ton.) As I arrived on the scene the players were about to take the field. The CO walked across to me. 'Know the rules of cricket do you, corporal?'

'I think so, sir.'

'Good. You can come out and umpire for us.'

I put on the white coat and took up my position at square leg. We were playing a neighbouring battalion whose CO came in to bat when the second wicket had fallen. After a couple of overs he went for a risky single. I was standing at the bowler's end. As the ball, flung by a fielder, struck the

76

stumps beside me, I adjudged that the opposition's colonel was six inches out of his ground. I raised my finger in response to a loud appeal. He walked towards the pavilion. Then our own colonel, fielding at square leg, bawled out, 'John . . . come back! You were well in!' Colonel John hesitated, then shrugged, and returned to the crease.

At this moment I made a decision. I was the umpire, the sole arbiter of who was out, and who was not out. If Colonel bloody Rotten wanted to take over my role, he was welcome to it. I walked slowly, unconcernedly, off the field. I knew that the cricketers would at first feel alarmed at my departure, then comforted in the knowledge that I was just going off to take a leak behind the big pine tree by the fine leg boundary. Except that I walked straight past it, and kept on walking, back towards the distant barracks, until I disappeared round the corner of the smallbore range, a lonely figure, but a man who was prepared to sacrifice all for the sake of a principle.

At least, that is what I intended. But for some reason my feet appeared to have grown roots. And after a few moments the bowler came on to bowl and the game was in progress once more.

REPORTING SICK

Every squaddie can expect to have some ailment or illness once in a while, but whether to get it treated or let it run its course is a matter for some cautious forethought. In the event of a broken leg or acute appendicitis there isn't too much option, of course. And there are other occasions when disability needs to be feigned, such as when a five-day survival exercise over the Brecon Beacons in mid-February is imminent. (See 'Skiving'.) The answer to such an eventuality is usually a slipped disc or a trapped sciatic nerve, or in the event of an attractive female physiotherapist being on the medical staff, a groin strain which requires massage can be an interesting variation. Knee trouble should be avoided though, otherwise they'll have your cartilage out in no time, and you'll be crippled for life.

One problem is that all medical staff believe that a soldier who reports sick with a complaint which has no outward and visible sign such as measles, is bound to be skiving. So if you've got a detached retina you're likely to be given a small bottle of eye lotion (with instructions to return any unused quantity) and passed fit for duty.

There are two basic types of medical officer in the British Army. If yours is a lieutenant in his late twenties who spends a lot of his time playing rugby, the chances are that he has had a bit of a struggle getting through his finals, and the senior tutor has taken him aside and suggested that rather than launch himself on the National Health Service, he should spend a year or two sharpening his skills on soldiers, who have no machinery available for complaints to the British Medical Association.

The other main category is the middle-aged captain. He will have had some twenty years' experience as a GP behind him, after which his partners in the practice will have bought him out, being somewhat alarmed at the frequency with which he is inclined to lift his elbow – especially before breakfast. There is a simple test for identifying an MO who is somewhat too partial to his tot. During inoculations he will invariably go for treble top and finish up in the area of double three. It's best to catch him as early as possible in the morning, and make sure you're first in the queue. Better still, don't go anywhere near him, unless you're in serious danger of snuffing it, and then only as a last resort.

During my own service, I only once reported sick. I had developed a rash of about a dozen unsightly looking warts on my left hand, and desired to be rid of them. The unit MO arranged an appointment for me to see the wart specialist at

the nearest military hospital. In the waiting room with me was one other warty patient, a private in the Army Catering Corps. He went in first. Ten minutes later he was carried past me, having passed out during the treatment.

I was called in. The specialist, a major, inspected my hand. 'Ah yes . . . well, let's see what we can do, hmmm?'

He picked up an electric needle and switched it on. The point began to glow cherry-red. He selected the second largest wart, on the base of my thumb, which was about the size of a pea. 'Let's start with this little chap, shall we?'

He plunged the needle in. It made a faint sizzling noise. An acrid whiff of burning flesh seared my nostrils. The pain was indescribable. As I throttled back a scream he observed, 'We all have to suffer to be beautiful.'

He excoriated a couple of smaller warts in similar fashion.

'Right, we'll leave it at that for today. Ask my clerk to give you an appointment for next week when you go out.' He tapped the king wart, which was about the size of a gooseberry. 'Then we'll have a go at the big fellow!'

Next morning when I woke up, I instinctively glanced at my left hand. It was completely wartless. The rest had all fled in terror.

FIZZERS

10542977 Trooper Wilshaw B. Is that your name and number?
   Sah!
   You are charged under Section 47(c) of the Army Act for damaging property in your billet, in that on the 17th of September, while you were billeted at 27 Marine Gardens, South Parade, Boscombe, you wilfully damaged a piano, and inflicted further depradations to the property of the proprietor, Mrs Ada Winstanley, of the same address.
   Sah!
   Staff Sergeant Crompton. What is your evidence?
   Sah! As NCO in charge of billeting I had a telephone call from Mrs Winstanley at 0850 hours on the 17th September. She informed me that a late night party had apparently taken place at 27 Marine Gardens on the previous day and she stated that at approximately 0125 in the morning she had heard the crunch of breaking glass accompanied by shouts of revelry. When she inspected the premises at approximately 0715 hours she discovered that her Broadwood piano had been damaged insofar as fragments of glass were lodged among the strings and there were beer stains all over the keys. She further complained that there was a trail of what she described as 'bobbles of vomit' proceeding from the sitting room to the front door which had inflicted considerable damage to the carpetry, and furthermore that an obscene message had been scrawled in lipstick upon an antique mirror advertising 'Old Grouse Whisky'. She estimated the cost of repairing the damage at £120. Sah!
   I see. Trooper Wilshaw. Is there anything you wish to say?

Er . . . well sir . . . y'see sir . . . I was just about to go to bed y'see sir, when there came this knockin' on the front door. Anyway . . . 'oo should walk in but Trooper 'Oskins with a crate of Pils and two young ladies . . . so anyway . . .

*

There must be very few squaddies, past and present, who have not been placed on a charge for some alleged misdemeanour or other. These little charades take place in front of the Company Commander, who plays the role of both prosecutor and judge. (There isn't any defence counsel.) One of the judge's close acolytes – usually a sergeant-major or NCO of his own staff – is the chief prosecution witness. The defendant is sometimes allowed to open his mouth to defend himself, at the judge's discretion, but is obliged to stand rigidly to attention like a stuffed penguin during the entire course of the proceedings. He is also divested of his hat and belt (just in case he should use one or other of these items to clobber the judge in the event of his not feeling too happy about the judgement).

The Army Act lists forty-five different offences for which squaddies can be charged. They encompass a wide variety of misdemeanours from malingering to mutiny. These were all put together about a hundred years ago by a committee of colonels and brigadiers who were surplus to establishment, since there was no important war going on at the time. But for the next fifty years or so, squaddies were always doing little annoying things such as being sick all over the regimental goat, which were not covered by the Act – and getting away with it. Eventually a captain who was leafing through the files came up with an unexpected brainwave.

'Why don't we have another category of chargeable offence,' he suggested, 'such as "Conduct to the prejudice of the good order of military discipline". That just about covers the lot.' The colonel who was in charge of his department swiftly adopted the idea as his own, and finished up as Chief of the Imperial General Staff. (The captain got no further promotion, and died in obscurity, without ever having another idea, of any description.)

When I was a young soldier, I became well-acquainted with being on fizzers and the experience was not much to my taste. I therefore made a resolution – that when I acquired a bit of rank I would not, under any circumstances, give comfort to the opposition by putting any of my fellow soldiers on a charge. It wasn't too difficult to maintain this resolve, except on one particular occasion. I was a sergeant at the time, and the battalion I was with had been warned for overseas service – at the sharp end. In order to get in some sort of shape for the campaign, we were sent to the wilds of Norfolk for a couple of weeks of intensive training. I was sent up with the advance party to help get the camp ready. Just before I left, I decided to inspect the .22 Mossberg rifles in the armoury and I took one away for 'further repairs'. There wasn't anything wrong with it, but I thought I might knock off the odd rabbit while I was sculling about in the undergrowth. So I took it down to Norfolk with me.

The situation there was almost terrifyingly rural – some thirty-odd rusting Nissen huts of Second World War vintage nestling in some fifty acres of elephant grass and bracken, surrounded by glowering woods.

After I'd been there a day or two I spent an evening prowling around this unfriendly territory with the Mossberg, but I didn't see a single rabbit. What I did notice was that the place was alive with pheasants, strolling around like chickens, chuckling from every bush. While it occurred to me to knock off a brace or two, I'd never plucked a pheasant before and didn't much fancy the experience. So I resisted the urge.

Next day a lance-corporal called Dolby strolled into the hut where I had established my quarters. Dolby, who was shaped like a pear with legs, belonged to the pioneer platoon and was in charge of the sanitary section, concerned with clearing drains. He noticed the Mossberg rifle standing against the wall.

'Ey sarge, is it all right if I take the rifle out and 'ave a go at a rabbit?'

I was engrossed in a book at the time, and can't have heard the question properly, or realised the identity of the supplicant. In the event, I nodded in vague acquiescence. Dolby took the rifle and the box of ammo beside it. About an hour later he stumbled back into the hut, his face as pale as a turnip.

'I ran into this big gamekeeper, sarge . . . 'e's took the rifle off me.'

I did a little urgent research, and found that the whole area enclosing the training camp was a vast game reserve owned by the local bigwig, Lord Saxmundham.

In the local pub that night I found out where the game-keeper lived, and cycled round to see him. He came to the door of his cottage – a Scotsman built like a Victorian wardrobe, with features of fumed mahogany which had re-

86

cently been treated for woodworm. I got nowhere. He waved the Mossberg triumphantly in my face. He'd got Dolby's name and number and was going to bring him up before the beak at the local Magistrates' Court. (Chairman of the bench, Lord Saxmundham.)

A couple of days later the rest of the battalion arrived, and I was compelled to report the circumstances involving the loss of the Mossberg rifle. It wasn't long before the RSM took me aside, and filled me in on the situation.

If the case went to court the rifle would be produced as evidence, and subsequently back-loaded to the War Office. Losing a weapon is a court-martial offence and some smart-arsed brigadier at the Warbox would be bound to want to know from the colonel exactly who was being court-martialled, and when. And, if the colonel couldn't produce the right answers, he would swiftly find himself transferred to the command of a pack of beagles somewhere in South Lanarkshire.

So, the RSM inferred, a head was due to roll. Either Dolby's, mine, or the colonel's. And it was most unlikely to be the colonel's. He gave me half an hour to stick Dolby on a fizzer for stealing and losing a rifle – otherwise he would charge me with the same offence.

I wrestled for some twenty minutes with this hideous moral dilemma. I'd always vowed never to put anyone on a fizzer. On the other hand one of us, either me or Dolby, was going to get shat upon from a vast height – and it was Dolby, after all, who'd got nabbed, and handed over the rifle to big Jock like a tame teddy-bear. I filled in the charge sheet. Dolby was notified to be on Company Orders next morning, at 1030 hours.

But I wasn't finished yet. I rang up the nearest police station and asked to speak to the inspector in charge. I gave him the full treatment. The battalion was about to go overseas, to a theatre of war, I said. A good few of the lads wouldn't be coming back. And just because some ignorant, pear-shaped sanitary mechanic had taken a pot shot at a rabbit, my commanding officer was in danger of being disgraced, and removed from his command, etc. I was almost sobbing when I'd finished. The inspector, who sounded like a decent sort of bloke, was sympathetic, said he knew Lord Saxmundham quite well and would have a quiet word in his eardrum. I was to ring him back at nine-thirty next morning.

I picked up the telephone at the appointed hour and rang the station. The desk sergeant said the inspector hadn't arrived but was expected any minute. I rang again at ten o'clock and got the same message. At 10.15 I called in at the company office, where the CSM was already lining up the accused and escorts, including Dolby. I asked him if he could delay Dolby's case. He said he couldn't, but there were six other squaddies on fizzers and he would march Dolby in last, which gave me about an extra twenty minutes.

At 10.20 I rang again. The inspector had just arrived. He said he'd just been to see Lord Saxmundham, and managed to persuade him to drop the case, much against his better judgement. The inspector implied that what had eventually swung it was that his lordship was a military man himself – he was Colonel-in-Chief to some local territorial mob, the West Norfolk Yeomanry or something, and he didn't really want to drop another colonel in the cess. So the gamekeeper had been instructed to deliver up the hardware, and keep his mouth shut about the whole episode. I could collect the Mossberg whenever I pleased.

I thanked the inspector and expressed the hope that he would finish up as Chief Constable, then whammed down the phone. I jumped into the Company Landrover and drove to the gamekeeper's pad like the clappers. He handed over the Mossberg with all the enthusiasm of a man who'd won the 10,000 metres at the Olympics, only to be told that he'd got to give the medal back because the team secretary had forgotten to sign his registration form. I got back to the company office as Dolby was being screamed at on the veranda, prior to being marched in. I waved the Mossberg in front of the sergeant-major, took the charge sheet from his reluctant fist, and tore it in half.

My honour was saved – at least until the next time!

CREEPING

This is a technique which is despised in most quarters but, nevertheless, it can be useful in extreme cases where one has to deal with particularly unpleasant superiors. It is largely concerned with an apparently cringing approach used when you want to get something out of them. The following formula has been known to be effective:

'Er . . . excuse me corporal/sergeant/sir . . . I was just wondering . . . only you see . . .'

A typical usage would be as follows:

'Er . . . excuse me sergeant . . . I was just wondering if it might be possible for me to swap guard duties with Palfrey on Thursday, only you see it so happens they're having the darts championships in the NAAFI on Thursday evening, and I'm in the doubles final.'

This offers the NCO the opportunity to practise his scintillating wit.

'I should 'ave thought there's only one final you could 'ave got to, Jenkins, and you don't need a dartboard for that.' This is followed by grudging acquiescence. 'All right, tell Palfrey to report to me . . . just this once, mind.'

It is sometimes difficult for a sensitive soldier to refrain from sneering during the recitation of this formula – a dangerous, and sometimes fatal error. It's also all too easy to become confused by prognosticating the words one would like to say, even while uttering the others.

'Er . . . excuse me sergeant . . . I was just wondering if I could poke my index finger up your hairy great snout . . . only you see it's one of my life's ambitions to cause you

serious embarrassment, if not actual physical pain. Er . . .
sorry sergeant, that was just a joke . . . I'll start all over
again.'

Flattery is also a useful weapon for softening up the opposition when all else has failed.

'That was a smashing goal you scored in the knock-out cup
last night, corp! I doubt if the goalkeeper even saw it.'

('We won't talk about the three open ones you missed and
the penalty you gave away. However did you get into the
team?')

I have to confess that on the few occasions when I resorted
to creeping the results were always less than satisfactory.

'Oh er . . . excuse me, sergeant. I thought that was a
remarkably good talk you gave us on the art of camouflage
yesterday. It was extremely lucid, and very much to the
point. I felt as if I was seeing the whole subject with entirely
new eyes.'

'Are you trying to take the piss?'

Perhaps I lacked conviction . . .

WOMEN

In their relationship with the opposite sex, soldiers are often accused of being sexist, chauvinistic, and 'only out for the one thing'. They are frequently reviled by feminists for categorising all women under the collective noun 'crumpet', and describing them in such terms as being 'all the same with a sack over their 'eads'. This is only about eighty per cent true.

On the other hand, if you were to take a census of all regular squaddies over the age of twenty-five, you would find that about eighty per cent of them were installed in married pads with a pram on the lawn and a Ford Escort in the driveway. So it must be assumed that, on the whole, the wenches are holding their own. Whereas of course the ideal is to wait until you're over thirty, with a sergeant's stripes up and a neat new XR3 in the car park, then select a little cracker of about nineteen as your future companion, and break her in to your ways.

Despite the advent of the Pill and the so-called Permissive Society, the basic situation hasn't changed a great deal over the last fifty years and most girls are still indoctrinated by their mothers' fundamental advice in sexual matters:

'Keep your 'and on your ape-knee.' (Especially where the army is concerned.)

Thus many squaddies still go through the agonies of two or three hours of spine-tingling French kisses in the long grass behind the recreation ground, without ever reaching the promised land – it's always promised for the next time.

'It's not as if I really know you, Don.'

Sober middle-class citizens who live in neat suburban villas on the fringe of a military camp will often glance through their windows over the corn flakes and discover that one of their garden gnomes seems to be sporting a floppy dunce's cap. They realise at once that a soldier has passed by during the small hours of the morning, seething with sexual frustration.

The chase is an interminable subject of conversation in the NAAFI bar afterwards:

''Ow did you make out with that little dark piece?'

'Bloody useless! One o' these intellectuals. All she could talk about was 'er brother passin' 'is soddin' 'A' levels. She went out eventually with some geezer who looked about forty. I was very chuffed to see the back of 'er. Ey, you crafty old bugger – that blonde thing you latched on to was a bit gorgeous. Did you manage to get your end away?'

'Nah – you'd 'ave to marry it first. But I stuck 'er on my list for future reference.'

Every sexually frustrated squaddie knows some smooth bastard in his platoon who looks like Robert Mitchum must have looked fifty years ago, who is getting his onions regularly. He's only got to walk into a crowded bar or a disco, and all the birds compete to catch his eye. The one he selects comes crawling on her belly, and within half an hour he's sorting her out in the back of someone else's car, which has got more room than his own. And he's always giving it chapter and verse afterwards, going into every explicit detail. Of course, the bloke's got no idea how to treat women – his brains are located in his chopper. Whereas that little blonde was quite a good conversationalist. Knew what she was talkin' about. Pity she 'ad to disappear early because of 'er Mum bein' in 'ospital.

Ah, stop kiddin' yourself. You saw 'er in the fish 'n' chip shop about an hour later with some orange haired punk civvy nitwit . . . right? She must be as dense as jellied pork, 'angin' around with people like that.

Still, I suppose it could 'ave been 'er younger brother . . .

Most garrison towns have their resident nymphos who supply the sexual needs of the local frustrated soldiery for nothing more than an evening's drinking in one or other of the local hostelries. These ladies usually become quite famous as they gradually develop into middle-aged doxies, unmarried but much loved, if only spasmodically, by battalions of partners down the years. Those I remember include Warminster Winnie, Blondie of Bulford, Catterick Katie, and Colchester's celebrated 'The Rabbit', who once nearly got a sergeant busted when he was caught by a sentry lifting her over the perimeter fence of Roman Way Camp at four o'clock in the morning.

I have always believed that these ladies deserve a medal, preferably to be presented by the local GOC in front of the town hall fountain, and attended by a guard of honour selected from all those, from corporal to colonel, whom she has serviced in the past.

'Carpark Annie of Aldershot, I hereby invest you with the Distinguished Conduct Medal in honour of your unflagging and dedicated service to the assorted soldiery of this town over the last twenty-five years, particularly in the teaching and training area, and in respect of your outstanding contribution to morale.'

OUT OF BOUNDS

In many overseas stations – particularly those east of Suez – a number of areas and particular establishments are out of bounds to other ranks. These include certain hotels and bars where officers, British businessmen and Embassy officials are prone to foregather in a 'home from home' sort of atmosphere. The reason for the ban is fairly obvious – officers are not keen to rub shoulders socially with the proles during off-duty hours.

Imagine a situation where a platoon commander is sitting in the smoke room enjoying a sundowner and a smoked salmon sandwich with his just arrived, rosy-cheeked little bride, the former membership secretary of Woking Young Conservatives, when who should walk in but one of his own section corporals with a stunning slit-skirted Chinese cracker on his arm.

'Oh good evening Mr Harvey, sir . . . evenin' ma'am . . . Erm . . . I don't think you've met Chi-Chi.'

But this is not a really serious problem, since most squaddies do not care, in their off-duty hours, to rub shoulders with boring expatriate British civvies, and still less their own officers, in cream-distempered hotel bars with phoney white-enamelled fans revolving in the ceilings, and little dishes full of frozen shrimps from Scarborough on the coffee tables.

What is much more inconvenient is that sometimes whole districts of large cities are placed off-limits, and these will invariably be the most exciting and exotic – the bazaars, the casbahs, the pulsating and multitudinous street markets, the narrow crooked alleys with their enchanting little cafés where you can magic half the night away under the glowing lanterns with a bottle or two of saké and a sinuous Eurasian piece.

Unfortunately, these areas also contain the red light districts, and the military hierarchy tends to be paranoid about the prospect of all the squaddies making a beeline for the knocking shops, picking up a dose, and dishing out a few military secrets while they're at it, such as the lock mechanism of the Vickers gun. Moreover, some officers have normal human characteristics, and it would be embarrassing if a company commander, mounting the rickety stairs, met one of his own men coming down:

'Ahm . . . Corporal Kitteridge! I've been looking for you everywhere! I suppose you realise that this place is out of bounds?'

'Sah!'

The answer to this is to adopt a disguise, possibly that of a European student running to seed in the tropics. First of all, learn a few sentences of German, from a phrase book, off by heart . . . 'Please leave me alone . . .' 'Why don't you mind your own bloody business, mein herr?' . . . etc. Then get your gear together – a pair of patched and frayed shorts, a scruffy old faded 'Oktoberfest 1979' T-shirt, a battered Tyrolean hat. Go down to the forbidden quarter, change your clothes in a public convenience, give your exposed flesh a coat of suntan and don the dark sunglasses.

For the rest of the day – and night – the town is yours. If you should happen to be addressed by one of your own kind, you simply utter a gutteral, and incomprehensible response, and pass on. In a shabby old green-shuttered tenement, murmurous with the voices of the indigenous inhabitants and stifling with the reek of grass and joss sticks, you will be awakened just before dawn when a corporal of the Military Police pushes through the wickerwork doorway of your bedroom and shines his torch in your face. He quickly withdraws as you snarl a Bavarian insult, and rejoins his companions on the landing.

'Not one of our blokes, then?'

'Nah . . . just 'Arry the Kraut and 'is chick.'

MARRIED PADS

When a soldier does eventually get clobbered by the female predator and embarks on the domestic procedures, some considerable thought should go into the organisation of the life style which the happy couple hope and expect to enjoy in the future.

In this context the occupation of married pads – the custom-built quarters for married soldiers provided by the army – should be avoided, unless the only alternative is an open sewer, or the top floor of the district headquarters of the IRA.

The problem with married quarters is their basic military uniformity. They are arranged at right angles in little housing estates. The names of the roads invariably have the ring of battles long ago – Malplaquet Avenue, Torres Vedras Close, Corunna Villas, Kumasi Drive. The matchbox gardens behind are very much of a muchness, and are required to be 'kept tidy' on pain of a sharp note from the Regimental Quartermaster Sergeant, which begins, 'It has been brought to my attention . . .'

The officers' married pads are somewhat similar, but detached and rather grander, with bigger gardens which are kept tidy by hired gardeners, paid for out of regimental funds.

Another drawback is that soldiers' wives in quarters tend to assume the rank of their husbands in relation to other soldiers' wives. This applies particularly to officers' wives. An adjutant's missis can be decidedly barbary towards the enamorata of second-lieutenants, and those of majors can get increasingly hoity-toity over a period of years of sustained boredom, towards all and sundry.

One way out is to marry a good-looking wench who just happens to have a typing speed of 150 wpm, an expert knowledge of word processors, and a cracking good job in the local town with the Halifax Building Society. A mortgage on a little cottage about five miles out of camp might then be considered. Such a move would naturally be regarded with the gravest suspicion, and it would be necessary to maintain a low profile for the next six months until the opposition got used to the idea.

SKIVING

Much of military life, particularly among its lower echelons, consists of tedious routine. This is because there is too much time around, and the surplus has to be consumed by non-productive activity. (The army would be just as efficient if it worked a 20-hour week.) All too often a corporal will be delegated to march a section of men a couple of miles away from the camp with instructions to 'find them something to do' for a couple of hours. If the corporal is unimaginative, he will sit them round in a little circle under an oak tree and conduct a quiz on the lines of who played in goal for England during the semi-finals of the World Cup in 1966. Or if he is more physically inclined he will have them hunting for four-leaved clovers.

Skiving is the art of taking short cuts through the tedium and discomfort. It is a necessary – even essential – craft which must be developed by every soldier.

To take a simple example. A new CO arrives at a unit, and in order to demonstrate the power of his personality, he declares that the personnel in the unit are pasty-faced and generally unfit. So for three days a week, every soldier under the age of forty has to get up in the misty dawn and go for a six-mile trot before breakfast, under the tender control of some jaunty PE sweat.

This one is not too difficult. After the first run, you hobble to the MI room and report sick with a ruptured hamstring, which stubbornly resists all treatment thereafter.

I had my first instruction in the skiving art from a rheumy-eyed veteran of thirty years' service over a pint in the NAAFI when I was the rawest of recruits. He advised me to coat my buttons with nail-varnish, rather than keep polishing them with metal polish.

He was most proud of his record in the Second World War – he'd served all through it as a storeman in some transit camp near Gosport, dishing out anti-gas equipment to heroes, coming and going to and from the sharp end, and he'd collected a large repertoire of other people's stories of action at the front.

Before this war he'd served for several years in India with some now defunct infantry mob called the Somerset Light Infantry.

'Day after day,' he told me, 'Us used to exercise on this dirty great plain. There was a little pimple in the middle called "One-Tree Hill", with this one little scrubby tree right on top.

'Us used to 'ave to train our mortars on 'un . . . zero our rangefinders on 'un . . . 'til we was bored out of our skulls.

'So one night me and one o' my mates got hold of an axe and we sneaked out and chopped the bugger down.

'We never trained there n'more. They never found out who done it, neither. They 'ad to change the name on all the maps.'

*

When I first became an armourer I was posted to a workshop, and I discovered that most of my time was consumed by inspecting endless racks of rifles. After a few weeks of this I became aware that my soul was beginning to shrivel, so I began to evolve a scheme designed to preserve it.

The examination and repair of a rifle involved eight specific tests. One of them concerned the cartridge headspace. You slipped a couple of gauges into the breech – one to be accepted, the other rejected. All of the first 500 or so rifles I inspected passed this test, so I decided it was not worth bothering with.

Similarly, I was supposed to peer through each barrel to

see if it was bent. Apparently a bent barrel casts a different shadow from a straight one, but I'd never learned to tell the difference, and they all looked the same to me. So I scrubbed this test too.

Within a few more weeks I'd got the eight tests down to three, but I still had trouble keeping up to my production target, as the bothersome ASM never failed to remind me. So I developed a new technique – I would only inspect one rifle in two. It was one of those brilliantly simple ideas. All I had to do was take a rifle from the 'uninspected' rack, give it a wipe with an oily rag to make it looked worked on, and transfer it to the 'inspected and repaired' rack.

After a couple of months I was inspecting one rifle in five, my output was the highest in the workshop, and I had all but mastered the techniques of the *Telegraph* crossword puzzle.

*

A good skiver will always be looking for the right opportunity, which can appear and recede quite rapidly – the advantage must be grabbed as soon as it presents itself. I recall one such occasion when I was at a REME workshops in Stirling. It was autumn and the leaves of the willows flanking the River Forth below the camp were beginning to fall into the water and drift towards the estuary.

It had just been announced that a visit from a minor royal personage was to take place on a date during the following June. The CO decided that in order to smarten the place up, he would have a thousand tulip bulbs planted in a large border flanking the flagpole outside the guardroom, ready to bloom in time for the royal visit. I was one of three squaddies selected to do the planting, under the direction of a rather dour and saturnine corporal.

It was a dank, drizzling sort of day in late October. The plot had already been prepared and manured. All we had to do was plant the bulbs in long straight ranks, like a platoon of guardsmen. The corporal handed out the bulbs, the little handforks, the stringlines, and the instructions.

'Right,' he said, 'Get cracking. I'll be back in a couple of hours' time and I'll want to see it just about finished by then. And make sure you do it properly or I'll 'ave your arses bendin' down 'ere until midnight.'

He then retired to stretch himself out on his pit with a bottle of Newcastle Brown and a girlie magazine – a thoroughly normal sort of bloke.

After the corporal had departed, the three of us held a brief conference. One of my companions, Craftsman Skelton – a hard man from Nottingham who'd served his apprenticeship in a Correction Centre – began to fulminate about the morality of the exercise. The CO, he complained, had bought the bulbs by raiding the funds of the Regimental Institute, which were supposed to be spent on facilities for the lads such as footballs and free contraceptives in the FFI hut. And here we were, supposed to be sweating our balls off and breaking our backs, spending our own money on providing a bit of bullshit for some useless bloody royal . . . etc.

The outcome of our deliberations was that we would plant the bulbs in the form of a rude word – or rather two rude words – right across the border. This used about four dozen bulbs. The remainder we planted in a big cluster between them, in the shape of a crown.

The exercise took some twenty-five minutes. We tickled up the rest of the plot with a rake to make it look worked over, then retired to the NAAFI for a cup of char and a shortcake.

But Skelton was too impatient a man to wait for the slow maturing of our protest. That same evening he fired off a bitter letter to the *Daily Mirror* protesting about the misuse of regimental funds. A few days later the story was featured on the front page.

The CO (following a tense little interview with the GOC, Scottish Command) was required to replace the money out of his own pocket. A week later Skelton was posted to the Orkneys, where he was given the job of repairing clapped-out lawn-mowers used by officers' wives. He wrote to me later and claimed that he'd managed to fix one or two.

He wasn't talking about lawn mowers.

During the following spring, I kept a close watch on the plot as the green blades began to spear through the surface. By the middle of May the message was becoming distinctly legible, although a couple of plants were missing in the 'K' of the first word, as were two or three in the final 'F' of the second.

Mice, probably.

Some three days before the royal visit, as the tulips burst into full bloom, their riposte was at last noticed by an eagle-eyed sergeant on a bicycle. Skelton of course was blamed, although the original idea was my own.

The CO, who was, after all, a man of some resource, decided to cut his losses. He allowed the large cluster in the shape of the crown to remain, but ordered the others to be picked on the morning of the event with the dew still fresh on the petals. They were presented to the Princess as a bouquet by the RSM's little daughter as she alighted from her Rolls in front of the guard of honour. She accepted them with practised grace and charm.

Nobody afterwards bothered to tell her what they had so recently spelt.

WORKING YOUR TICKET

Soldiers who enlist in the regular army may well find that after having tested the water – say for six or seven weeks – the military life is not quite their cup of cocoa, and they would prefer to chance it back on the dole queue. Unfortunately there is the little matter of the five or six remaining years of their regular engagement still to be considered.

There are a number of ways in which a soldier can be discharged before the end of his allotted span. One of them is discharge by purchase, but not many soldiers can scrape together enough ackers for this expensive operation. Moreover, a large section of the army is disbarred from even applying. And even among those who are permitted to apply, the General Officer Commanding can (and often will) put the mockers on their ambition on the grounds that the applicant is essential to the efficiency of his unit. This may not be strictly true. It depends rather more on the side of the bed from which the general has emerged on the day the application is presented for consideration. It's also a waste of time applying for this way out if your unit has just been warned for overseas service, particularly if it's at some place where a war is going on.

There is discharge with ignominy, but this means of escape can only be awarded by a court martial, and in order to achieve it the soldier must first of all commit some ignominious act such as assaulting the provost sergeant. Even so, such an exit would inevitably be preceded by six months in the Colchester glass house, an experience which is up nobody's street.

Technically, one is supposed to be allowed out by standing as a candidate in a parliamentary election. But the CO would be unlikely to look favourably on an application to appeal to the constituents of Humberside West on behalf of the Cheaper NAAFI Prices Party.

It's also possible to get discharged on medical grounds. Physical incapacity is rather difficult to swing – flat feet have been tried in the past but it's unlikely you'd have been let in with these in the first place. Mental disorders are much easier to simulate and have known to be successful on a number of occasions. A Private Swinbank, in my experience, tried to work his ticket in this way. He went to his sergeant major and complained, 'Sir, there's something going on in my head.' The CSM not unnaturally replied, 'Well, that's got to be an improvement, lad.'

'No sir, something keeps goin' round and round.'

'Well, why don't you stick a knittin' needle in your bloody ear'ole, that'll stop it.'

Swinbank had to put up with this sort of unsympathetic treatment for several months, until he eventually got to see a psychiatrist, who decided that someone who wanted to get out of the army so desperately as to feign mental illness must have a serious problem, and recommended his discharge on the spot.

But perhaps the discharge category to aim for is 'Retention undesirable in the interests of the service'. You begin by ordering a daily copy of the *Morning Star* from the local newsagent, and in off-duty hours you are seen ostentatiously reading it. When interest has been aroused, you acquire a large poster proclaiming 'Brits Out of Ireland', and paste it on the door of your locker. The next step is to prepare a petition demanding that a trade union branch should be formed in your battalion, and you offer your services as shop steward. You point out all the advantages this would bring. Any soldier who found himself on a fizzer would have a union representative to defend him. The local union commit-tee would negotiate with the adjutant on such matters as pay

110

increments, working overtime, sickness benefit, and any disputes arising from differing interpretations of Queen's Regulations. You then forge about sixty names of your fellow soldiers underneath, including corporals and sergeants and perhaps a sergeant-major or two. You present the petition to the Commanding Officer, not bothering to wait for an interview, but simply barging into his office and thrusting it under his nose.

They will give you twenty-four hours to pack.